My First Book of Prayers

A Collection of Everyday Prayers from a Child's Heart

Illustrations by Maureen Bradley

An Inspirational Press
Book for Children

Compilation copyright © 1997 Lion Publishing
Illustrations copyright © 1993 Maureen Bradley

This edition first published in 1997 in the USA
through special arrangement with Lion Publishing by
Inspirational Press, a division of BBS Publishing Corporation,
386 Park Avenue South, New York, NY 10016.
Inspirational Press is a registered trademark
of BBS Publishing Corporation.
Library of Congress Catalog Card Number: 97-71140.

ISBN 0-88486-181-3

All rights reserved. No part of this work may be reproduced or
transmitted in any form or by any means, electronic or mechanical,
including photocopying, recording, or any information storage and
retrieval system, without permission in writing from Lion Publishing Plc,
Peter's Way, Sandy Lane West, Oxford OX4 5HG, England

Printed in India

Everyday Prayers

Father, we thank you

Father, we thank you for the night,
And for the pleasant morning light;
For rest and food and loving care,
And all that makes the day so fair.
Help us to do the things we should,
To be to others kind and good;
In all we do at work or play
To grow more loving every day.

In the morning

Heavenly Father,
you have given this new day to me.
Help me to make it one that pleases you
by doing my best in everything,
because I love you.

Thank you

For this new morning with its light,
Father, I thank you.
For rest and shelter of the night,
Father, I thank you;
For health and food,
for love and friends
for everything your goodness sends,
Father in heaven, I thank you.

At school

Thank you, God, for this new day
In my school to work and play.
Please be with me all day long,
In every story, game and song.
May all the happy things we do
Make you, our Father, happy too.

A happy day

Loving Father, on this day
Make us happy in our play,
Kind and helpful, playing fair,
Letting others have a share.

For those who suffer

Lord Jesus, I pray for those
who will be unhappy today:
For parents who have no food
to cook for their children;
for parents who cannot earn
enough money for their families;
for children who are sick or frightened;
and for those who are alone
and without people to love them.

A busy day

Thank you, God, for the daytime
when I can be awake and busy.
Thank you for all there is
for me to do today:
new things to find out,
friends and games to play with.
Thank you for the sun
that gives us warmth and light
to see by.

For animals

Dear Father, hear and bless
Thy beasts and singing birds,
And guard with tenderness,
Small things that have no words.

Make me like you

Lord of the loving heart,
May mine be loving too.
Lord of the gentle hands,
May mine be gentle too.
Lord of the willing feet,
May mine be willing too.
So may I grow more like thee
In all I say and do.

You love us

Thank you, Lord Jesus,
that you love us the same today
as yesterday.

Everyday Graces

Thank you

Thank you for the world so sweet,
Thank you for the food we eat.
Thank you for the birds that sing,
Thank you, God, for everything.

Eating with a crowd

Bless this bunch
As we munch our lunch.

A harvest grace

All good gifts around us
Are sent from heaven above.
Then thank the Lord,
O thank the Lord
For all his love.

For simple meals

The bread is warm and fresh,
The water cool and clear.
Lord of all life, be with us,
Lord of all life, be near.

A grace to sing

For health and strength
and daily food,
we praise your name,
O Lord.

Thanks for all our food

For every cup and plateful,
God make us truly grateful.

A Jewish blessing

Blessed art thou, O Lord our God,
King of the Universe, who bringest
forth bread from the earth.

For food and drink

For food and drink and happy days,
Accept our gratitude and praise;
In serving others, Lord, we do
Express our thankfulness to you.

An invitation

Come, dear Lord Jesus, be our guest,
And bless what you have given us.

A Chinese grace

Each time we eat,
May we remember God's love.

God is great

God is great, God is good,
Thank you, God, for all our food.

Prayers for Special Days

On a special day

Thank you, God,
for special days to look forward to,
and special days to remember.

Sunday

For this new Sunday with its light,
For rest and shelter of the night,
We thank you, heavenly Father.
Through this new week but just begun,
Be near, and help us every one
To please you, heavenly Father.

A happy day

Thank you for each happy day,
For fun, for friends, and work and play;
Thank you for your loving care,
Here at home and everywhere.

Today

Dear Lord Jesus, we shall have this day
only once; before it is gone, help us to do
all the good we can, so that today is not
a wasted day.

My birthday

O loving God, today is my birthday.
For your care from the day I was born
until today and for your love, I thank you.
Help me to be strong and healthy,
and to show love for others, as Jesus did.

When we are ill

Lord Jesus, I am ill.
Please make me well.
Help me to be brave
and thankful to the people
looking after me.
Thank you for being here with me.

When I do wrong

Dear God, thank you that you love me.
I'm sorry that I sometimes do things
you wouldn't like, or which hurt others.
When I do wrong, help me to own up quickly
and to tell you that I'm sorry.
Thank you that you're always so willing
to forgive me.

Vacations

Thank you, God, for vacations
In the lovely summer days,
For our picnics, for our fun,
For our playing in the sun.
Make us good, with smiling faces,
So our homes are friendly places,
And the helpful things we do
Make our parents happy too.

Autumn days

Thank you, our heavenly Father
for harvest time:
for ripe fruit in the orchards
and berries in the hedges;
for the vegetables and all the food
gathered in and stored for winter days.

Christmas

It's nearly Christmas,
when it's Jesus' birthday.
Thank you, God, for baby Jesus.

Easter

Good Friday is a time of sadness,
Easter is a time of gladness.
On Good Friday Jesus died,
But rose again at Eastertide.
All thanks and praise to God.

Goodnight Prayers

By day and night

Father, unto you we raise
Hearts and voices full of praise.
Bless us waking, guard us sleeping,
Through this night and all our days.

When I'm frightened

Dear God, sometimes
I get frightened at night.
Please look after me tonight.

At night

Glory to thee, my God, this night
For all the blessings of the light;
Keep me, O keep me, King of kings,
Beneath thy own almighty wings.

A bedtime prayer

Jesus, tender Shepherd, hear me;
Bless your little lamb tonight;
Through the darkness please be near me;
Keep me safe till morning light.

All this day your hand has led me,
And I thank you for your care;
You have warmed and clothed and fed me;
Listen to my evening prayer.

My friends

Thank you, God, for my friends;
We've had such fun today.
I can hardly wait for tomorrow
when we next go out to play.

For children everywhere

O God, our heavenly Father,
bless and keep your children
all over the world,
this night and for ever.

Jesus, friend of little children

Jesus, friend of little children,
Be a friend to me;
Take my hand and ever keep me
Close to thee.

Sorry

Loving Father, I'm sorry for the wrong things
that I have said or thought or done today.
I'm sorry if I made others unhappy,
but most of all, help me to be sorry
if I have hurt you.

In bed

Now that I'm sleepy, God,
I thank you for bedtime stories,
for my warm, cosy bed and
for someone to tuck me in at night.

Never alone

In our work and play God leads us,
Every step we take.
In our sleep he will be near us,
Watching till we wake.

On a moonlit night

The moon shines bright,
The stars give light
Before break of day;
God bless you all
Both great and small
And send a joyful day.

Acknowledgments

We thank those who have given us permission to include prayers in this book and apologize for any copyright omissions.

Cassell plc: from *The Infant Teacher's Prayer Book* by D.M. Prescott (Blandford Press), 'Thank you God, for this new day'.

Church Missionary Society (CMS): from *All Our Days* by Irene Taylor and Phyllis Garlick, 'Thank you, God, for holidays'.

Concordia Publishing House: from *Little Folded Hands*, 'For food and drink and happy days' and 'God is great'.

Ladybird Books Ltd: from the former Ladybird title *The Ladybird Book of Prayers through the Year* by H.I. Roston, 'Thank you, our heavenly Father'.

Zinnia Symonds: from *Let's Talk to God* by Zinnia Bryan, 'Thank you, Lord Jesus, that you love us', 'Lord Jesus, I pray for those...', 'Thank you, God, for the daytime' and 'Loving Father, I'm sorry for all the wrong things'; and from *Let's Talk to God Again* by Zinnia Bryan, 'Lord Jesus, I am ill'.

SPCK: from *A Brownie Guide Prayer Book* by Rosalie Wakefield, 'For this new Sunday with its light'.